Table of Contents

The Genesis of Ash Wednesday

The Mother's Tears and Abraham's Dust
Augustine's Insight on Ash Wednesday

by

Dr. ant

3

Copyright 2024 Dr. ant. All rights reserved.

No part of this book may be reproduced in any form or by any electronic or mechanical means including information storage and retrieval systems, without permission in writing from the author. The only exception is by a reviewer, who may quote short excerpts in a review.

Although the author and publisher have made every effort to ensure that the information in this book was correct at press time, the author and publisher do not assume and hereby disclaim any liability to any party for any loss, damage, or disruption caused by errors or omissions, whether such errors or omissions result from negligence, accident, or any other cause.

This publication is designed to provide accurate and authoritative information with regard to the subject matter covered. It is sold with the understanding that the publisher is not engaged in rendering professional services. If legal advice or other expert assistance is required, the services of a competent professional should be sought.

The fact that an organization or website is referred to in this work as a citation and/or a potential source of further information does not mean that the author or the publisher endorses the information the organization or website may provide or recommendations it may make.

Please remember that Internet websites listed in this work may have changed or disappeared between when this work was written and when it is read.

The Mother's Tears and Abraham's Dust: Augustine's
Insight on Ash Wednesday

Contents

Introduction: Penitence and Piety in Augustine's Time

In the annals of Christendom, the epoch wherein Saint Augustine strode the earth was a crucible of spiritual fervor, wherein the depths of sin and the heights of sanctity commingled. 'Twas a period where the contours of early Church doctrine were shaped amidst tumultuous debates and fierce introspections. As we embark on dissecting the fabric of such an era, we find that penitence and piety were not merely aspects of religious decorum but vital strands interwoven into the very essence of Christian life.

The rippling influence of Augustine's own journey—a path that saw him traverse the terrains of hedonism and emerge into the light of divine grace—is indelibly etched into the practices that define the Church today. His thoughts on penitence vermilion threads in the ecclesiastical tapestry, mark an evolution from ancient ritual to heartfelt contrition.

Central to the observances of this period was the sacramental grace that flowed through the act of penance, cultivating a landscape abundant with the language of repentance. It's within this confluence of earthly failings and heavenly aspirations that

Augustine's reflections resonate; his teachings gleam like beacons illuminating the pathways towards God's merciful embrace.

Divine intercession is epitomized in portrayals of sacred figures across scriptural texts; Augustine's exegetical work embraced this dynamic robustly. He construed Old Testament passages as foreshadowing the Christian requisites for true contrition and viewed the acts of figures such as King David—his penitential psalms especially—as archetypal for Christian remorse and redemption (Pratt, 1903).

In Augustine's purview, penance wasn't solely a private undertaking; instead, it was interlaced with the communal fabric of the Church. His explications enshrined the idea that collective acknowledgement of transgression could lead to profound unity in seeking divine pardon.

The resonance of Augustine's spiritual ethos is palpable when considering the universal signs of penitence—most conspicuously, in the ritualistic imposition of ashes. His influence colors the rite not as a mere tradition but as a symbol potent with meaning and a gateway to human humility before God's majesty (Kaufman, 1982).

To fathom Augustine's weighty contributions to penitential doctrine, one must delve into the zeitgeist of his day—a time enshrouded with profound grappling between sin and righteousness. Augustinian thought elucidated the inexorable link between man's fallen nature and the sanctifying grace that beckons through penance.

The textured understanding of such ancient piety cannot be overstated; it's through

Augustine that one discerns the nascent forms of religious practices that now feel timeless. His portrayal of our mortal coil as a pilgrimage back to Our Creator is etched in his homilies and texts, which remain pivotal in Church teachings and personal meditations on divine forgiveness.

A cursory glance at Augustine's influence reveals an intricate intersection of theology, human psychology, and cosmology, reflecting the truths that penetrate the human soul's encounter with the divine. His reflections offer an oracular voice on the disparate elements of human experience and a yearning for reconciliation with God.

Situated within the throes of a collapsing Roman Empire, Augustine's musings on penitence and piety are replete with poignant relevance for the faithful. Just as he addressed the afflictions of his contemporaries with pastoral sensitivity, his words speak through time, guiding today's pilgrims toward the hallowed ground of repentance and conversion.

As such, in contemplating penitence and piety in Augustine's time, we unravel a thread that connects the consecrated practices of yore to our contemporary quest for righteousness and absolution. It is a time-traveled dialogue between Augustine and ourselves, unfolding the eternal human predicament of sin and our ceaseless pursuit of God's redemptive grace.

This inquiry shall be confined for now to the broader context of Augustine's era; to the brimming wellspring from which flowed his profound insights on the human condition, and the essential acts of humility that align mankind with the divine will.

In becoming attuned to the complexities of penitence and piety in the times of Augustine, one is summoned to reflect upon one's own spiritual journey, measuring it against the yardstick of ancient wisdom that continues to inform our modern expressions of faith.

Thus, it is with ardent expectation that we proceed, exploring the ancient terrains of the human heart laid bare in Augustine's ruminations, to grasp a more profound understanding of how

penance and piety shaped, and indeed continue to shape, the life
and legacy of the Christian journey towards sanctification.

The Genesis of Ash Wednesday

In the commencement of our ecclesiastical calendar, behold the venerable tradition of Ash Wednesday, whence the faithful are marked with ashes, symbolizing a return to the very dust from which mankind was first wrought by the Creator's hand (Smith et al., 2019). This first chapter doth aim to unravel the historical threads that converge upon the genesis of this solemn day, tracing its lineage back to the customs of old and their eminence in Holy Scripture. We shall eschew later elaborations, focusing earnestly on the ritual's nascent form, unearthing its pertinence in the context of early Christian acts of penitence. It is here we find ourselves amidst the ethos of repentance, which shaped the reflections and teachings of the early Church Fathers, yet we shall not delve deeply into the thoughts of Augustine here, for this treatise reserves his meditations for ponderance in the chapters that ensueth. Behold, the ritual of ashes stands not as an emblem of eternal condemnation, but rather as a palpable reminder of mankind's fallible nature and the merciful grace that beckons unto a pilgrimage of penance, culminating in the resurrection promise of the
Paschal feast (Connell, 1998).

The Ritual of Ashes as we traverse further down the path once trodden by our spiritual forebears, we encounter the solemn practice of receiving ashes. This rite, a conspicuous reminder of the frailty inherent to our mortal coil, reverently marks the beginning of Lent, a penitential season within the Christian liturgical calendar. It stands as a stark symbol not solely of our demise but of penitence and the ceaseless cycle of death and rebirth to which the faithful are called.

Fashioned from the remnants of palms blessed in the previous year's Palm Sunday celebrations, the ashes themselves are an Artifact bearing witness to triumphant and humble glories alike. In the act of imposing these ashes on the congregants' foreheads, the church whispers a poignant reminder: "Remember that thou art dust, and unto dust shalt thou return" (Genesis 3:19). These words, a somber echo of the Genesis narrative, invoke the essential truth of human origin and end.

This ancient ritual, preserved through centuries within the bosom of the Church, serves not merely as a sign of mourning or contrition. Rather, it bears the dual weight of despair and hope, imprinted upon the faithful as they acknowledge their sins yet anticipate the cathartic purification that lies ahead. Like a phoenix rising anew from the ashen heap, the Christian spirit is invited to undergo a transformation, shedding the decay of sin to embrace the vivifying presence of the Holy Spirit (Ferguson, 1979).

Our ruminations upon the ritual extend further to the biblical antecedents of this act. Ashes and sackcloth were the garb of prophets and people alike when connoting grief, penance, or mourning for transgression. To don ashes was to be visibly penitent, to rend one's heart in the sight of God (Joel 2:13). The ashes therefore act as a conduit, a tangible medium through which the faithful assume the penitent's mantle.

The contemporary enactment of this ritual palpably connects the individual to the collective history of the community of believers. Across nations and epochs, those who tread the path of repentance have received upon their brows the same mark, a continuity of tradition that transcends individual experience. This shared somatic symbol serves to unite us, reflecting our common heritage in Adam and shared destiny in Christ's redemptive sacrifice.

In the gentle application of ashes, the faithful encounter a tactile juxtaposition between the holy and the profane. They are invited to partake in shared humility, recognizing in themselves the same dust that was once animated by the Divine breath of life (Genesis 2:7). This solemn ceremony, therefore, is a harbinger of the journey each soul undertakes toward sanctification, as it meanders through Lent towards the cleansing sanctity of Easter.

Partaking in this ritual, one is paradoxically marked for isolation and inclusion. To bear the ashen cross upon one's brow in the public square is to outwardly profess an inward grappling with one's own sinfulness. Yet in this public display, the individual finds unity in the ecclesial body, a fellowship of sinners seeking redemption.

The ashen cross, writ upon the forehead, represents a tangible intersection where personal narrative meets the salvific narrative of Christ. The cross, emblematic of Christ's victory over death, reminds the penitent that through death comes life, and in acknowledging mortality, one grasps at the promise of immortality.

Implicit in this rite is a call to conversion, a turn from worldly distraction towards the divine. Ashes signal a reorientation of priorities, desires, and aspirations towards the eternal and the holy. The external act of accepting ashes mirrors an internal commitment to renew one's life in Christ, a resolve to enter fully into the spirit of Lent with its disciplines of fasting, prayer, and almsgiving.

Thus, the ritual of ashes ushers us into a solemn observance, a holy season marked by introspection and purification. It compels the heart to consider not merely the inevitability of earthly demise but also the grandeur of divine mercy. We are reminded, through this unpretentious substance, of our creation from and return to the earth, but also of our redemption through Christ's paschal mystery.

Let us, therefore, approach the ritual of ashes with a demeanor of reverence and humility, cognizant of its profound symbolism and its place within the tapestry of our faith tradition. Let it be an outward testament to an inward grace, the beginning of a Lenten pilgrimage that prepares the soul for the joyous celebration of the Resurrection.

In sum, the Ritual of Ashes stands as a threshold to introspection. It calls forth a commitment both personal and communal to engage in the Lenten voyage. As we submit ourselves to the smudge of mortality, we embark on a transformative endeavor, punctuated by the disciplines of the season and sustained by the hope of Easter's renewal. Thus begins the Christian's expedition from the perishable to the imperishable, ordained by the sacred scriptures, and consecrated through centuries of solemn ritual.

Echoes in Augustine's Writings As we delve into the rich fabric of Augustine's oeuvre, one is immediately struck by a persistent resonance – a motif that traces its origin to the sacred rite of Ash Wednesday. Augustine, whose voice still echoes through the annals of time, imparts upon us a profound understanding of penitence, nestled within the broader context of divine grace and human frailty. It's through his various works that one discerns the shadow of ash, symbolizing our mortality and our yearning for redemption.

The eminent bishop of Hippo was not one to shy away from the corporeal reality of death, nor the vestiges of sin. In his "Confessions," Augustine lays bare the tumults and tribulations of his soul, an introspection that mirrors the contrition palpable in the Ash Wednesday rite. 'Remember that thou art dust, and to dust thou shalt return' – this memento mori is indelibly imprinted upon Augustine's narrative of conversion, a constant reminder of human transience and the need for repentance.

In "City of God," Augustine situates the human condition between the burgeoning City of God and the waning City of Man. The dust and ash of Ash Wednesday are emblematic of our citizenship in the city of Man, yet they also pave the way for the heavenly city. Augustine's discourse on the two cities elucidates the stark duality of existence – where the ashes bear witness to our sinfulness, yet also herald our potential for sanctification.

Through the luminous veil of his sermons, Augustine's reflection on the penitential season of Lent provides further insight. He elucidates the theme of renewal – a metamorphosis evoked by the solemn reception of ashes. It's a call for humility, where one acknowledges personal shortcomings before God yet is also reminiscent of the Genesis account wherein mankind was fashioned from dust (Screech, 1990).

In deciphering Augustine's epistles, we discover his continuous call to spiritual sobriety, a motif congruent with the Ash Wednesday ethos. Augustine admonishes the faithful to shed the superfluous and turn towards the austerity that better unites the soul with its Creator. This echoes the Lenten journey – commencing with ash – moving from earthly attachments towards divine contemplation.

The theological treatises of Augustine, brimming with exegetical profundity, touch upon the narrative of the Fall. Here, Augustine explores humanity's mire of sin and the subsequent promise of salvation – a theme inextricably linked with the symbol of ashes, which signify both the consequence of sin and the hope of pardon through Christ's Passion.

Furthermore, Augustine illuminates the intimate relationship between repentance and grace. Though mankind is mired in sin, symbolized by the ashes of Ash Wednesday, divine grace can restore the soul to its original splendor. In his works on grace, Augustine underscores the primacy of God's mercy, which like the cleansing of ash, absolves sin and renews the spirit.

An examination of Augustine's moral philosophy reveals a consistent thread of temperance and self-restraint, virtues that align with the self-denial and moderation indicative of the Lenten season. It's a reminder that through the ritual of ashes, we commence a passage of self-denial, as means to spiritual enrichment and alignment with the divine will.

Delving into the narrative of Augustine's "De Civitate Dei," reveals the temporal nature of the world, akin to the transient quality of ashes that are brushed away. Throughout this treatific vision, Augustine's vision of humanity's destiny is steeped in a sense of impermanence, urging believers to look beyond the ephemeral to the eternal.

When Augustine ponders the plight of human suffering in his homilies, he often highlights its redemptive potential, much like Ash Wednesday which symbolizes the transformative power of suffering when united with Christ's own. It's within such suffering that Augustine finds a call to a deeper faithfulness and a more sincere form of witness.

In his commentary on the Psalms, Augustine's expositions frequently allude to themes of repentance and purification, akin to the very essence of Ash Wednesday. His deep reflections encourage the faithful to see in their own lives the dispossession of the sinful self, transitory as ash, and to embrace a spiritual rebirth.

Augustine's profound grappling with the notion of original sin in his anti-Pelagian writings also echoes through the ritual of Ash Wednesday. The ash reminds us of our fallen nature and our shared heritage of sin which Augustine argues only divine grace can redeem.

In the quietude of Augustine's prayers, as presented in his "Soliloquies," one encounters a personal conversation with God. In these intimate exchanges, the sensibility of Ash Wednesday infuses his speech – humbly acknowledging human limitation and seeking divine wisdom for purification and guidance.

While exploring the intricate thoughts of Augustine, it's clear that the tradition of Ash Wednesday finds its reverberations throughout his writings. Though not explicitly devoted to the ritual, his texts convey kindred themes that are evocative of the ashes bestowed upon the faithful – a symbol of mortality, humility, repentance, and ultimately, the hopeful transition towards salvation.

In the summation of our inquiry into Augustine's reflections, we see the palpable presence of Ash Wednesday's philosophical and theological underpinnings. Augustine's musings remind us that from dust we were created and to dust, we shall return, but it is through penitence and divine grace that our journey finds meaning and our souls aspire to the eternal city beyond the ashes of this world (Thompson, 1948).

Chapter 2: The Talmudic Tapestry

In the unfolding of "The Talmudic Tapestry," one must gaze upon the intricate interlacing of Judaic wisdom with Christian understanding, as it was perceived through Augustine's contemplative eye. This second chapter casts its regard upon how the Talmud, a comprehensive body of Jewish lore and law, contributed threads to Augustine's theology, thereby enriching the fabric of Catholic belief with patterns of ancient tradition. As the roots of an olive tree entwine deeply within the soil of God's chosen land, so too does Augustine's philosophy intertwine with the profound sentiments of rabbinical thought, transposing the echoes of Solomon's Proverbs and the ethical precepts of the Pharisaic sages into the tapestry of Christian sentiment. The essence of penance, a theme recurrent in Augustine's musings, shall herein be traced back to its Talmudic origins, where it was preached as an indispensable element for spiritual atonement and deliverance, a veritable foretaste of what one discovers in the fullness of Augustine's writings. 'Tis through exploring such a weft of interfaith dialogue that one may unveil deeper comprehensions of penitential praxis and its implications on the soul's reconciliation with the Divine.

Augustine's Assimilation of Jewish Wisdom As we venture forth from the Talmudic tapestries that grace the timeline of scripture, one cannot, in good conscience, set aside the impact of Jewish wisdom upon the venerable Augustine. The sagacity emanating from the Proverbs of Solomon, the lamenting poeticisms of the Psalms, and the enduring narratives of the Torah have painted their indelible strokes upon his intellect and spirit.

In consideration of this learned church father's union with Hebraic thought, it is essential to acknowledge that his apprehension of scripture was never of an isolated manner. Augustine beheld the ancilla of Jewish wisdom as a guide to divine truths. This foundation fortified his perspective, which hath blossomed into voluminous works espousing the depths of Christian reflection and piety (Lowenstein, 2002).

Verily, his appropriation of Jewish sapience steered him to discern the nature of the Almighty in His creative works. It was the Jewish ethos of wisdom, epitomized in the figure of Solomon, that imparted to Augustine a fascination with order, knowing, and the unfolding of divine revelation.

The incorporation of Jewish exegesis within Augustine's writings served not only to elevate the practice of penance within the Christian community but also to draw succor from the very roots of Abraham's bosom. Thus, it is with due diligent inquiry we might trace back to those proverbial parallels in

Proverbs where the fear of the Lord is but the beginning of wisdom (Proverbs 9:10).

For instance, his treatises resonate with echoes of Ecclesiastes, where the preacher's call to remember one's Creator found a profound ally in Augustine's exhortation to recall our mortal nature. This motif agrees well with his teachings on the sobering application of ashes, symbolizing penance and the passing nature of earthly life.

Moreover, Augustine's contemplations on the Psalms are rife with the fruits of Jewish liturgical prayer, wherein the piety of David's heart pours forth in Augustine's own appeals for divine mercy, grace, and forgiveness. He couples these pious reflections with a philosophical rigor that situates them firmly in the dialogue between faith and reason.

Augustine surmised that penance is hardly a mere moral reckoning, but it is an invitation to return to Eden's innocence, a sentiment thoroughly Jewish in its longing for restoration and reconciliation. In such manner, he utilized the Jewish understanding of repentance—as a turning back to God—to impart a powerful message of conversion and renewal.

Consider his "Confessions," which can be perceived as an embodiment of the introspective and confessional aspects of the

Psalms, Jewish prayers that intimately reveal the heart's tumult and triumphs before God. It is through this prism that one discerns Augustine's theological dependencies on Judaic structures of thought and devotion (Cardin, 2000).

Furthermore, the Jewish theme of remembrance, a thread woven steadfastly through their history and feasts, is adopted by Augustine as he enjoins Christians to remember their past bondage to sin, and to cherish the liberating sacrifice of Christ. This Christian appropriation of an essential Jewish practice speaks volumes of Augustine's philosophical and theological synthesis.

As Augustine traversed the Old Testament, he dearly esteemed the narrative of Joseph. This Jewish exemplar of virtue and forgiveness showed Augustine that true wisdom lies in the discernment and governance of one's life according to God's graceful plan.

The humility exemplified by the Jewish sages, particularly that of Moses, became for

Augustine a mirror into the soul's journey towards God. He admired Moses, who had seen God face to face, yet remained the meekest of men—an ideal in the call to Christian penance.

Augustine's musings on the story of Job, a tale steeped in Jewish tradition, painted a vivid portrait of suffering and steadfastness that served as a beacon to those seeking God amidst the trials and tribulations of their temporal existence.

In the Law and the Prophets, Augustine found a treasure trove of precepts and prophecies, aligning them with Christ's teachings and further enriching the discourse on contrition and conversion. The narrative of the Jewish people, estranged by sin and then reconciled by adherence to the Law, found a new expression in Augustine's advocacy for a life renewed through penitence.

Finally, the wisdom literature of the Jews adorned Augustine's thought and is perennially manifest in his sentiment that Christ is the veritable Wisdom of God (1 Corinthians 1:24); hence, all true wisdom finds its summit and fulfillment in Him. Augustine's theological discourse is thus permeated with the profound recognition that the locus of Jewish wisdom has, through Christ's revelation, been transfigured and made manifest in the fullness of divine Light—the very same Light that illumines the path of every penitent soul towards salvation (Neusner, 2004).

In summation, the synthesis of Augustine's Christian wisdom was not bereft of the rich tradition of his Jewish forebears. By assimilating these ancient strands of reflection, contemplation,

and devout practice, Augustine forged a legacy that has stood
the test of time, nurturing faith's journey in the hearts of
believers unto this present day.

The Archetypes That Prefigure Penance

In tracing the lineage of penitential practice, one must excavate the layers of historical sediment to reveal archetypes prefiguring the Christian understanding of penance. In the Hebrew scriptures, long before the conception of Ash Wednesday and the Christian liturgical practices, there lay stories that served as nascent expressions of the penitential spirit. The tendrils of this spirit weave through the Talmudic tapestry, offering both foreshadow and foundation to Augustine's later exegesis.

One sees Cain, after his grievous act against Abel, driven to wander the earth in penitence, bearing the mark of both God's judgement and protection (Genesis 4:15). This act of divine mercy in the face of sin alludes to the tension therein between God's justice and His mercy; the first echoes of a doctrine of penance can be heard in the distant beat of a fratricide's heart.

Further along the sacred chronicle, one encounters the figure of King David, whose psalms are wrought with the expressions of a contrite heart. In his penitential Psalm 51, David avows, "Create in me a clean heart, O God; and renew a right spirit within me" (Psalm 51:10 KJV). This plea for spiritual cleansing and renewal parallels the Christian penitent's journey from ashes to the hope of resurrection.

The Prophet Isaiah speaks of penitential themes as well, urging the people to "Seek the LORD while he may be found; call upon him while he is near...Let the wicked forsake his way, and the unrighteous man his thoughts; and let him return unto the LORD, and he will have mercy upon him" (Isaiah 55:6-7 KJV). This call to return (in Hebrew, shuv) prefaced the later Christian call to metanoia, a transformative change of heart.

Jonah's sojourn into the heart of Nineveh stands as a testament to the power of repentance. Scripture recounts not only Jonah's own reluctant journey towards obedience but also the collective penance of a city veering from impending destruction through sackcloth and ashes (Jonah 3:5-10).

Across the variegated collection of wisdom literature, one finds the Book of Proverbs instilling an early wisdom that chastises the soul towards the path of righteousness, reiterating the virtue of humility—another cornerstone of penitential theology—as pivotal in the proverb: "Before destruction the heart of man is haughty, and before honour is humility" (Proverbs 18:12 KJV).

The narrative of Job is illustrative as well, charting the traverse of an innocent sufferer from prosperity to affliction and, crucially, to a place of dialogue and restoration with the Almighty. His story is replete with the motif of dust and ashes (Job 42:6), presaging the symbolic expression of human frailty and repentance integral to Ash Wednesday and the liturgical legacy of Augustine's era.

These vibrant threads from the Hebrew scriptures form a tapestry of lessons prefiguring the penitential disposition later inscribed into the rites and reflections of the early Church. These are the shadows from which light will later spring, the sketches anticipating the full portrait of Christian penance. It is within the loom of this tradition, the people of God found themselves arrayed in the rough garments of lamentation, signifying through external acts the internal posture of contrition.

Moving from the Jewish texts, one glimpses the penance-laden stories emanating from the

Apocryphal books, often underappreciated within the corpus of Christian exegesis. The Prayer of Manasseh is a poignant example, with its elaborate confession and call to God's inexhaustible mercy, captured in the supplicant's cry, "O Lord, Almighty God of our fathers,
Abraham, Isaac, and Jacob, and of their righteous seed; who hast made heaven and earth..."

(Prayer of Manasseh 1:1)

Similarly, in the narrative of Judith, the heroine's humility and acts of self-denial presage the role of personal sacrifice in the Christian understanding of penance. Her deeds were not merely individual acts but were communal in nature, contributing to the salvation of her people and reinforcing the social aspect of penance. Judith's story, with its coursing motifs of fasting, prayer, and the evocative use of ashes, vividly foreshadowed the communal practice of penance and its salvific potency.

Even when transposing these ancient echoes to Augustine's frame, it is vital to acknowledge that within them is a pulsating awareness of personal sin and communal suffering. They understood sin not merely as individual transgressions but as blemishes upon the collective holiness, calling for collective restoration. As these archetypes find their fuller interpretation in Augustine's thought, they bear on them the vestiges of a communal identity in which the act of penance is both personal pilgrimage and collective voyage.

It was upon the shoulders of these narrative giants that the theology of penance would eventually surge forward, finding robust expression in the patristic age. Augustine, with a keen eye for the scriptural past and its figural interpretation, recognized in these archetypes the primordial gestures of a humanity in search of divine absolution. They informed his understanding of the human need for penance and God's grace in the sacrament of reconciliation. Augustine's intellectual prowess, steeped in the study of these ancient exemplars, led him to a deeper wisdom about the nature of sin and the imperative of penance.

Thus, Augustine's writings on penance were not simply novel theological musings; they were built upon an enduring narrative tradition, a lineage of sacred storytelling that traced the arc of human fallenness and compel the soul towards conversion. In recognising this, one discerns both the continuity and the innovation in Augustine's insights: while he anchored his teachings on the bedrock of scriptural precedents, he unfurled new layers of understanding tailored for the Christian heart and its longings (Kim,1991).

In conclusion, the archetypes that prefigure penance provide a rich tapestry from which Augustine and the Christian tradition at large draw. These scriptural narratives not only illuminated the path toward penance for the early Church but also established enduring patterns that resonate within the contemporary faith journey, guiding the penitent's steps from the shadows of the Old Covenant into the luminous embrace of the New.

Chapter 3: Abraham's Dust: Humility and

Remembrance

In contemplation of Abraham's dust, we uncover the timeless lesson of humility, a truth deeply woven into the sacramental tapestry of penitence. To engage with the scriptural narrative is to be reminded of the mortal state unto which even the patriarch of faith, Abraham, was bound, and whence he cried, "I am dust and ashes" (Gen. 18:27). This somber reckoning echoes through ages, calling the flock to a reflective sojourn in the transient world wherein humility and remembrance stand as dual beacons. As the faithful traverse the landscape of Lent, chastened souls recall that from dust they came and to dust they shall return, embracing the precedence of contrition in the footsteps of the penitent Abraham. Theological scrutiny unveils a poignant bearing upon the dust of Abraham as an emblem of our humanity, predisposed to frailty, yet summoned to divine fellowship. Such remembrance renews the spirit, yielding to a profound awareness that life's transience is but a passage to the immortal communion with the Creator, as exemplified in Abraham's covenant with God (Almen, 2003).

The Patriarch of Faith and His Path of Sorrow

In the shadowed annals of sacred history, there tarries the tale of a man whose footsteps through the dust of Canaan echo unto the hearts of the faithful in these latter days. Abraham, venerated as the patriarch of faith, trekked upon a path beset with sorrow, a path which brings forth illumination upon the nature of penitence and piety. His sojourn was fraught with trials, binding his heart ever closer to the Divine, even as the weight of impending sacrifice bore down upon his aged shoulders. Indeed, the story of Abraham is a tapestry interwoven with threads of trust and tribulation, of submission and sorrow, facing the inexorable demands of faith.

To ponder deeply is to perceive that Abraham's journey conduits much more than the historical odyssey of a solitary soul; it delineates the contours of a spiritual archetype. He was summoned forth from the familiar to the unforeseen, from the land of his fathers to a realm promised by the voice of God. This very abandonment of the certain, this rending of the heart's tapestry in favor of divine providence, marrows the essence of penance. Through his life's narrative, the perils of the flesh are vanquished by the fortitude of belief, rendering unto Abraham the countenance of steadfastness amid strife.

The binding of Isaac—Abraham's promised son, the very fructification of God's covenant— endows the patriarch's tale with its most grievous sorrow. As the wood was ladened upon Isaac's back, mirroring the cross to come, Abraham's fidelity to God faced its crucible. For is it not in the offering of one's own promised future, in the deference to that which transcends comprehension, that the profundity of human trust in the Almighty is made manifest?

In this, the Zohar elucidates with mystical fervency, espousing that Abraham's willingness to sacrifice his son was the ultimate testament of faith, which in its agony, burgeons forth redemption for generations (Zohar, II, 33b-34a). Through this act of submission, Abraham's sorrows were not only his own but became a prelude to the redemptive sufferings of the Messiah, who would also carry the wood, who would also be offered—yet this offering would not be stayed.

The travail of Abraham is a microcosm of the human soul's journey towards the ineffable. Each step upon the barren earth, each starlit promise grasped in the solitude of night, brings one closer to the divine embrace. The anguish of Abraham encapsulates the fundamental truth that sorrow is oft the gateway to spiritual exaltation, and penance a vessel through which the soul may ascend.

Yet, even as this sui generis trial unfurled, Abraham's heart knew the consolations of divine fidelity. His was a sorrow interjected with revelations of God's steadfast presence. In Abraham's dialogue with God, one discerns a reciprocity; a covenantal bond that holds even in the heart's nocturnal hours,

bespeaking God's insurmountable grace in human fragility
(Bancroft, 1866)

In Abraham, the notion of remembrance converges with
humility, for to recall God's promises is to submit to a power
beyond one's own. As ashes signify mortality, Abraham's dust-
swept pilgrimage signifies humanity's transient state and the
humility that must accompany the recognition of one's own
finitude (Cowley, 1881).

Thus, within the paradigm of penance, Abraham's experiences
excavate the dualities of suffering and solace, offering an
exemplum for the faithful. His tears, while signalling anguish,
are also droplets that nourish the spiritual roots deep within the
parched soil of the human condition.

As each Lenten season ushers in a time of reflection upon the
sorrows of the sacred, so too are the faithful enjoined to cast
their gaze upon Abraham, patriarchal paragon of penitential
sorrow. Herein, his path of sorrow is not a road to be shunned
but rather embraced, for within his affliction lies the seed of
immeasurable grace—and in the shadowed depth of sorrow, the
light of understanding may yet be found.

And so, the church, e'er a sentinel to the truths revealed in
sacred scripture, upholds the narrative of Abraham as both a

historical constancy and a spiritual allegory. His path of sorrow, emblematic of the penitential journey, beckons the believer to a contemplation of faith's complexities, of sacrifice's necessity, and ultimately, of the hope that undergirds the contrite heart.

In the silent prayers and ashen crosses of Ash Wednesday, Abraham's legacy endures. His journey of faith underpins the gravity of the Lenten pilgrimage—wherein the faithful, like Abraham, surrender to the exigencies of faith, and discover therein the paradoxical liberty and the boundless mercy that follows.

As the patriarch of faith traversed his path of sorrow, so too do the children of promise walk in the shadow of his testament. Bearing the cross of the present moment, they find solace in the knowledge that the trials of this world are but fleeting, and the promise of God endures eternal. Thus, in the reflective heart, the sorrowful way becomes a conduit of hope, and the journey of penance, a passage to paradise restored.

In conclusion, the path trodden by Abraham speaks of a sorrow not borne in vain; it is the sorrow of he who sees beyond the veil of tears, trusting in the goodness of the Lord. His story, inscribed in the bedrock of faith, shall outlast the ages—as it pertains to mortals weathering the storms of existence—it stands as an

eternal symbol of humanity's arduous yet hopeful voyage
towards redemptive love.

Augustine's Exegesis on Abraham's Journey As we tread softly into the milieu of Augustine's interpretation of Abraham's journey, it becomes evident that the patriarch's sojourn is not merely an expedition through the terrestrial realms, but rather a metaphor for the spiritual pilgrimage of humankind. In Augustine's eyes, Abraham's wanderings were not solely historical notations but unveiled a blueprint for the passage from sin towards redemption.

In scrutinizing the text of Genesis, Augustine observed the call of Abraham as more than a divine directive to change his geographic locale; it was, in essence, a summons to embark upon a new mode of existence. When Abraham is instructed to leave his country, kin, and father's house, Augustine discerns a call to abandon the old self, to forsake the attachments of worldly living, and to step out in faith to the land that God would show (Gen. 12:1). The physical detachment mirrors a spiritual severing, a penitential gesture of forsaking past transgressions and embracing a state of grace (Norten, 2024).

A pivotal moment for Abraham, and for Augustine's exegesis, is the covenant between God and Abraham. This covenant, described as an everlasting covenant in Genesis 17, was wrought with symbols and portents that Augustine understood as prefigurations of Christ's New Covenant. Through tending to their sorrows and sins, Augustine saw how believers could partake in their own covenant with God, facilitated by penance and prayer, and ultimately leading to forgiveness and reconciliation.

As Abraham's travels took him through various trials and tribulations, Augustine also recognized parallels in the Christian's sanctifying journey. The trial of parting from Lot, a test of Abraham's love and trust in God's provision, was for Augustine an allegorical lesson on the detachment necessary for spiritual growth. The willingness to part with temporal goods, represented by Lot choosing the lush Jordan plain, served as an emblem of the inner penitential process (Jay,1988).

The profound moment of Abraham's testing with his son Isaac held a significant place in Augustine's interpretive framework. In the binding of Isaac, Augustine perceived an exemplar of God himself and His sacrifice of His only begotten Son. The wood that Isaac carried up Moriah's mount foreshadowed the cross Christ bore. The striking parallel could not be clearer, and to Augustine, Abraham's obedience mirrored the penitent's submission to God's will, even when it seems to lead to the death of what is dearly held.

Augustine further expounded that Sarah's barrenness and subsequent birth of Isaac was emblematic of the apparent futility of penance which nonetheless culminates in the joy of salvation. Sarah's laughter upon prophetic news of her child was a testament to the incredulity that besets the sinner when faced with the boundless mercy and transformative power of God (Levering, 2013).

Hagar and Ishmael's casting out was another potent event that Augustine saw through the lens of spiritual purgation. He argued it was symbolic of the necessary rejection of carnal desires and earthly attachments for one's spirit to be free to accept the divine inheritance promised through faith and penitence. Such is the plight of the believer in their journey through Lent and beyond, Augustine supposed.

Likewise, the destruction of Sodom and Gomorrah offered Augustine an analogy for the purifying wrath of God, cleansing the soul as fire clears brimstone from the earth.

Abraham's intercession for the city, with its gradation of righteousness, proposed a progression of penitential intercession, evoking the idea that even the most sin-laden souls could find redemption through earnest prayer and repentance.

In the tale of Abimelech, king of Gerar, and Sarah, Augustine found a complex interplay between fear, sin, and divine protection. Even as Abraham's fear led him to deceit by saying Sarah was his sister—a sin that threatened integrity—the grace of God intervened to prevent further transgression. To Augustine, this was another sign of how divine mercy operates amidst human frailty—and how the penitential path always allows for redemption and restoration of right relations with God.

The purchase of the burial plot at Machpelah, in Augustine's contemplation, signified the believer's acceptance of mortality; penance hence became a means to prepare for a life beyond the transitory. This act of securing a place of rest before his death mirrored the soul seeking its final abode through the purisome work of penitence.

Throughout Abraham's sojourn, Augustine was keen to note the presence of angels who guided and communicated divine intentions to the patriarch. To Augustine, these celestial messengers spoke to the reality of heavenly aid available to the penitent. They reflected the idea that, even as Abraham was guided by divine envoys, the faithful are also assisted by God's angelic forces as they navigate the penitential pilgrimage towards Easter's dawn.

Finally, Augustine's exegesis on Melchizedek, the king of Salem, tied Abraham's journey back to Christ. As Melchizedek blessed Abraham and shared bread and wine, it prefigured the

Eucharist, the ultimate sacramental penance and participation in Christ's sacrifice.

Augustine saw this encounter as a testament to the truth that the end of penance is always communion with God and partaking in the divine nature.

Amid these reflections, it becomes manifest that Augustine sought to weave the history of Abraham into the wider tapestry of salvation history—a passage from the dust of penitence to divine grace's embrace. For him and for those who tread in his interpretive footsteps, Abraham's journey is a template, telling of the arduous, yet grace-filled path that weaves through sorrow and culminates in the joy of Easter resurrection.

In essence, Augustine's exegetical work on Abraham's narrative was a profound rumination on the spiritual dynamics between man, sin, and God. His insights offer a rich reservoir for the contemplative, leading one to consider the depths of penance, the breadth of forgiveness, and the heights of celestial promise. The journey is arduous, yet it is trodden under the guidance of divine grace, which transforms even the most wayward of pilgrims into heirs of the everlasting covenant.

Chapter 4: Blessed Mother Mary: The

Quintessence of Sorrow

In the preceding discourse, the narrative of Abraham's descent into humility and remembrance did set forth a mirror to the forthcoming contemplation upon the Blessed Mother Mary. Indeed, she who is the epitome of sorrow, whose heart was pierced by the very sword of her own Son's suffering, bears the grace and agony of the world in her immaculate compassion. Her dolors must be hence comprehended not merely as a series of plaintive events but as profound emblems in the story of redemption. The Mater Dolorosa stands at the juncture of divine sorrow and human frailty, manifesting a theological fulcrum which allows mortals to glimpse into the profundities of shared suffering as means of divine grace. Her silent tears are akin to the ashes which the penitent don on their foreheads, symbolizing the transformative power of penance, a memento both of our earthly passage and spiritual ascent. As Mary's Seven Sorrows weave into the Lenten fabric, they bring forth an enigma of sanctity born from anguish, nurturing within the faithful a deeper veneration for the salvific journey towards the Paschal Mystery (Ewing, 2016).

Mary's Seven Dolors and the Ashen Cross

In the voyage through the annals of penitence and devotion, we must now turn to the profound mysteries enshrined within the Seven Dolors of Mary, and the relation of such piercing sorrows to the emblem of the Ashen Cross. The Ashen Cross dost not merely signify human mortality but also encompasses a profound interconnection with the lamentations of the Blessed Virgin. The dolors that pierced her heart are akin to the ashes that mark the faithful on the commencement of Lent, symbolizing both mourning and penitence.

Fathom, if thee will, the first dolor: the prophecy of Simeon, wherein he espake that a sword would pierce Mary's own soul (cf. Luke 2:35). The same foreboding prelude is reflected in the ashen mark upon our foreheads; 'tis a promise of the trials and tribulations each soul must bear, akin to the heaviness that lay upon Mary's heart.

The flight into Egypt, Mary's second dolor, betokens the pilgrimage of the soul toward salvation. Just as she fled with her infant Son to escape Herod's wrath, so must we retreat from the vice and sin into the wilderness of self-denial and prayer during the Lenten season, our faces marked by the Ashen Cross.

The third dolor, which saw Mary seeking her lost Son for three days, mirrors the spiritual desolation many a believer endures. In the discovery of Jesus in the temple, there lies a twining of joy and sorrow, much like the dual nature of Ash Wednesday—wherefrom springs hope in the midst of repentance, and joy even as the ashes remind us of the gloom of our sins.

With the fourth dolor, we perceive Mary meeting Jesus on the Via Dolorosa. Just as our foreheads are marked with the Cross, she beheld her Son bearing the very instrument of His Passion. Herein, our own crosses we bear throughout the journey of Lent find their prefiguration in Mary's sorrowful encounter.

The fifth dolor, witnessing the crucifixion of Christ, immerses the heart in the depths of Mary's grief. The sacrificial Lamb, upon whose body would lay the iniquities of us all, is gazed upon by His mother, whose suffering is ineffable. The Ashen Cross we bear is but a faint shadow of the cross that Mary witnessed on Calvary's hill.

Mary's sixth dolor calls to mind the unendurable: the Pieta, the Mother cradling her lifeless Son. Even as we receive the ashes, might we fathom her anguish? The stark reminder of death's reality is etched not only on our brows but also echoed in Mary's silent suffering.

The seventh dolor, the entombment, compels the faithful to contemplation on the finality of death and the impermanence of earthly life. Mary's surrender of her Son to the tomb resonates with the somber rite of Ash Wednesday, where ashes bespeak the dirge,
"Remember that thou art dust, and unto dust shalt thou return."

The tradition of honoring Mary's Seven Dolors invites a deeper understanding of the intersections between her sorrow and the Ashen Cross carried by Christians seeking to purify their hearts through penance. Each dolor encapsulates a particular anguish that, when meditated upon, nurtures compassion and humility—virtues eminent within the season of Lent.

Indeed, Mary's role as Mater Dolorosa and her intimate association with the Ashen Cross serve to fortify the faithful's resolve to walk the penitential road. She becomes a paradigm of unwavering faith and hope amidst suffering, guiding us through our own Lenten wilderness towards spiritual renewal. Her dolors, each a meditation on the cost of salvation, inspire awe and reverence in the devotee unravelling the sacred paschal mystery. The stories of Mary's sorrow are woven into the very fabric of the Ashen Cross, binding her experiences to the initiation of our Lenten journey.

Let us consider, as we bear the Ashen Cross, the measure of devotion that graced the heart of Mary through her dolors. It is through her travail that we may apprehend the profoundness of Christ's Passion and heed the call to conversion. In embracing the path of Mary's sorrows alongside the solemnity of the Ashen Cross, Christians re-discover the call to be ever-like the Blessed Mother—patient in suffering, resolute in hope, and steadfast in love.

In conclusion, the nexus between Mary's Seven Dolors and the Ashen Cross draws the penitent into a contemplative embrace with the sorrows of the Blessed Virgin. It is a convergence that beckons the faithful towards a deeper empathy with Mary's heartache, reminding us of our own capacity to bear our crosses in the reflection of her fortitude and grace. Thus, we enter the Lenten season marked by ashes, not in desolation, but in solemn solidarity with Mater Dolorosa, whose grief sanctified the very notion of sorrow through divine love.

Intersecting Paths of Maternal Grief and Lenten Grace

As the thread of Lenten piety weaves through the devotional zeitgeist of Augustine's era, so too does the visage of maternal sorrow, most poignantly personified in the Blessed Virgin Mary. The intertwining of Mary's grief, which reached its crescendo at the foot of the Cross, and the solemnity of Lenten grace provide a rich tapestry of contemplation for the pious faithful. This intersection beckons believers to a deeper engagement with the passion narrative and the salvific pain its players endured (Jones, 1997).

The viscerality of Christ's Passion bespeaks not only His suffering but also that of His mother. Analogously, the penitential season of Lent urges the faithful to consider their personal Golgothas. The grief Our Lady bore is echoed in the penitential ashes marking the faithful's foreheads, a reminder of mortality and sin's gravity that attunes the spirit to the sacred heartache of the Mater Dolorosa (Finely, 2004).

It is worthy to note the Sancta Mater's grace in her sorrow, as sorrow without grace is but despair. Unto this spiritual paradox doth the season of Lent speak: by grace, to find joy in mourning, strength in weakness, and resurrection in death. This mysterious paradox, akin to that which enshrouded Mary, serves to sanctify the penitents' passage through the reverent obscurity of Lent (Gertsman, 2012).

Verily, the incandescent moments of Marian dolor thus shine forth as signals of hope unto those in the Lenten pilgrimage. Beneath her mantle, the faithful are invited to partake in the bittersweet conjoinment of suffering and sanctification, the very facets of Christian calling wrought through the Passion of her Son (Cameron, 2012).

In the shadowed vale of Lent, how can one not call to mind Mary's silent courage? Her exemplar submits itself to us as an objurgation to advance, with due reverence, toward the restoration that lies yonder these forty days of atonement. For in her grief, chiseled by divine providence, lies the prelude to grace.

Consider, then, this intersection as a diptych of devotion, wherein the penitent grasps the very sorrows of the Mater Afflicta and thereby finds solidarity in supplication. For as sorrow shared is halved, so too is the aggregation of sin's weight made less by communal contrition. In her Son's prophecy fulfilled—"Behold, thy mother!"—the faithful are bequeathed an inheritance of grief transfigured by grace (Onongha, 2013).

The Marian visage, steeped in the dolor of a sword-pierced heart, does not repel but rather seduces the soul toward emulation. It beckons emulation not of despair, but of holy sorrow—an attentiveness to the cost of redemption, a cost divinely borne but humanly felt in the stings of maternal love and the ashes of Lent (Gertsman, 2012).

Reflecting upon the Simul Iustus et Peccator, one confronts the nature of man, at once righteous and sinner. So reflect we upon Mary, the stainless Mater Dei, acquainted inordinately with suffering. The conundrum therein is the coexistence of sin and holiness within us, a riddle explicated through a communion with her anguish, drawing grace as she did amidst immense woe.

Lent's austerity and the grayness of its days become mere shadows when contrasted with the deeper hues of Mary's tribulations. As the Covenant's Ark, she carried not just Christ but also the collective faith hope of a fallen people—the burden of which can scarce be comprehended, save through the prism of Lenten reflection.

So doth the mystery of ineffable love emerge, resplendent in sorrows of both a mother and her children chosen by grace. As the phoenix rises anew from the dumal wastes, so too do hearts riven with contrition find resurgence in the Marian exemplar, a phoenix of divine maternity (Satterfield, 2001).

The confluence of Lent and Mary's sorrows reveals a journey of internal exile and divine companionship, a passage through deserts of the soul toward a promised land of Easter's joy. This passage is pregnant with the realization that, in emulating

Mary's fidelity in anguish, the Christian too can embrace sorrows as path to resurrection.

In the Levitical specter, one discerns the prefiguration of penitential practice—an inclination that finds consummation in the Lenten experience. Mary's sorrow, like Lenten penitence, facilitated purification; an offering of the heart, rent with grief, yet unyielding in its hope of salvational deliverance. Thus, the culmination of maternal dolor and paschal tide sanctifies even the stoniest of hearts (Van Bavel, 1997).

Herein lies the testament: the Lenten sojourner, through Mary's tears, glimpses beneath the veil of suffering the countenance of mercy. The Believer's journey thereby transmutes the grief-stricken soil of Marial despair into a seedbed of salvific grace, every tear a rill of redemption overflowing the once-barren valleys of the soul (Connolly, 2002).

As the corpus of Lent draws toward its terminus in the triumph of Resurrection Sunday, the parallels between the broken-hearted mother and the penitent must not go unmarked. For as Mary stood by believing in the midst of despair, her heart rent asunder, so too the faithful must abide the trials of Lent with faith anchored in the surety of Easter morn.

In the convergence of Our Lady's lamentation and Lent's solemnity, the believer discovers an alchemy of divine love—a love encompassing the profundity of a mother's pain and the redemptive power of a grace-infused penance. This interweaving, this sacred intersection, stands as an enduring call throughout centuries to all who bear the ashes of humanity in pursuit of divine beatitude (Rosenfield, 1963).

Chapter 5: The Tears of Eve and Mary's

Lament

In the annals of the faith, the melancholy of Eve in her expulsion from Eden beareth a weight akin to the dolor of Blessed Mary, as she beheld her son's cross at Golgotha. The Tears of Eve, shed in the shadow of the fruit once grasped in disobedience, did proclaim the sorrow of humanity, whilst Mary's lament, pure and unsullied, spake of a world redeemed through sacrifice (Plantinga, 2000). Eve's tears watered the ground cursed by her fall; in contrast, Mary's did mingle with the blood of the New Adam, sanctifying the earth anew. In the compendium of salvific history, the locus of penance findeth its epitome in Mary's sorrowful heart—an embrace of penitence that reunites, in hallowed reflection, the tears of the first mother with the pains of the New Eve. And thus, traversing from the garden of sin to the mount of the skull, we expend our contemplations upon the rending aspect of Eve's disobedience and the balm of Mary's submission to the divine will (Van der Merwe, 2014).

From Eden to Golgotha: Sin, Suffering, and Salvation Dwell we now upon the narrative so ancient, the journey from Eden's verdant sanctuary to the brow of Golgotha, where redemption's price was dearly paid. In the recounting of this tale, let us consider the profound mysteries of sin and its begetting of suffering, as well as the supreme act of salvation that arose out of such travail. To divine this path is to understand the bedrock upon which penance and reprieve are constructed and the role that Most Blessed Mother Mary plays within this spiritual continuum.

Indeed, the transgression in Eden did rupture the harmony that was man's natural inheritance; disobedience introduced sin into a pure world (Bucur, 2008). From this juncture forth, suffering became an inextricable part of human existence, a consequence of the taint that humans bear. Yet, despite the shadow cast by original sin, a promise of redemption shimmered through Biblical prophecy, foreshadowing the path to Golgotha, where ultimate salvation awaited.

As sin begat suffering in this world, so too did it necessitate sacrifices for atonement. The blood of lambs and the fragrance of burnt offerings filled temples as symbols of a contrite heart seeking reconciliation with the Divine. These ancient practices prefigured the one perfect sacrifice to come, a cleansing flood to wash away the stains of iniquity for all time.

In the fullness of time, the scripture's prophecy incarnated in the person of Jesus Christ, the lamb without blemish (Cardin, 2000).

His sojourn on Earth was marked by suffering - a sharing in humankind's pain and a foretaste of His ultimate act of love. Christ's affliction was not just physical; for He bore the weight of all sin upon His soul, tasting the bitterness of alienation from the Father that man's iniquity had wrought.

And what of Mary, the Blessed Virgin, the one declared full of grace? Her heart was pierced by a sword of sorrow, a Mater Dolorosa, as she experienced the unfolding of salvation's bitter cost. Her lamentations at the foot of the cross were but an echo of Eve's anguish, manifesting a participation in redemption's price, her maternal heart joined in the salvific act of her Son.

Suffering in itself, it must be noted, does not redeem; it is but the crucible that may lead to purification and sanctification. It is in the acceptance of our crosses, the embracing of the divine will, that suffering transmutes into a means of grace, much like the blood that flowed on Golgotha's hill (McInerney, 2017).

Salvation, therefore, cannot be seen as simply freedom from suffering; it is the transformation of suffering into a testament of divine love. Salvation history bespeaks God's enduring commitment to humanity, despite the vicissitudes of sin, always offering a path back to grace—that celestial Eden from whence humanity first strayed.

As we reflect upon this history, we discern a tale of two gardens: Eden, where the first sin severed the bond between the Creator and the created, and Gethsemane, where the New Adam accepted the chalice of suffering for the sake of humanity's restoration. In both, a choice was presented; yet, the outcomes of these choices have defined the course of history for mankind.

The Via Dolorosa, the sorrowful way walked by Christ toward the site of crucifixion, represents not just a physical path of torment, but a spiritual journey through the valley of sin's consequences. At each station along that path, the depths of human frailty and the heights of divine mercy are starkly illuminated.

Indeed, the cross on Golgotha stands as a paradoxical symbol, an instrument of torture transformed into an emblem of hope. For upon that rough-hewn timber, death was vanquished and life everlasting was procured for the children of Eve. Salvation's tree had borne its fruit in the resurrection, which followed upon that dark Friday's sacrifice.

Retrospection reveals the arc of God's plan, a narrative that stretches from the first whispers of humanity to the thunderous declaration of the empty tomb. It speaks of a Creator unwavering in pursuit of His creation, of a love so profound that it would endure the cross, the grave, and the harrowing of hell to reclaim that which was lost.

In the wake of redemption's dawn, mankind is invited to participate in this salvific act through the sacraments, especially in the rite of penance. In confession and absolution, the supplicant is invited to lay down the burdens of sin, and akin to pilgrims journeying to a holy sepulchre, find renewal and hope in the mercy that is without end (Schneiderman, 2008).

Contemplating the path from Eden to Golgotha imparts a lesson of intertwining sin and grace. For humans, beneficiaries of salvation, the task is to delve into the mysteries of this journey, to find in every tear shed by Eve or Mary, in every drop of blood shed by Christ, the echoes of the divine call to repentance and renewal.

As we partake in Lenten observances, the echoes of this sacred history resonate, reminding us of the potency of penitential practices. These acts serve to join our own sufferings to the salvific work of Christ and honor the Blessed Virgin's sorrows as integral to God's unfolding plan of redemption.

Thus, from Eden to Golgotha, from the garden to the grave to the glory of resurrection, spans the story of human disobedience and divine salvation—a narrative encapsulated in the journey

that sinners tread toward salvation, a trek that finds its
terminus and triumph at the empty tomb and beyond.

Augustine's Reflections on the Role of Women in Salvation History In our contemplative journey through the annals of salvation history, as chronicled by Augustine, one finds the handiwork of the Almighty intricately woven with the filaments of feminine virtue and obedience. Forthwith, the role of women in the divine narrative is not merely ancillary, but rather central to the unfolding of God's redemptive plan.

Certainly, Augustine perceived the account of Creation, epitomized in the tale of Eve, as an allegory rich with implications for understanding salvation. Eve, though eternally bound to the Original Sin, partook also in the prophecy of redemption, whence she was denominated by our forefather as "the mother of all living" (Genesis 3:20). Thus, her parturition represents not solely the advent of sin, but simultaneously the inception of a salvific lineage.

Articulating Eve's role in the antecedent stages of human history, Augustine postulated that through her seed would come the New Eve, she who would defy the serpent and crush its head with her seed, who is Christ. Herein, the role of women becomes clear: They are vessels of the sacred, conduits through which the Saviour of men would enter our world, as foretold in the hallowed scriptures.

Through this exegeses, Augustine adumbrates a further testament of women's significance in the saga of salvation, as illuminated through the figure of Sarah, wife of Abraham. Sarah's barrenness and subsequent miraculous conception symbolize the divine intervention and the fecundity of grace, foregrounding the eventual Virgin Birth of the Messiah (O'Connell, 1996).

However, it is within the figure of Mary, the Mother of our Lord, that Augustine's meditations ascend to their zenith. The Virgin Mary is adored as the immaculate vessel, the Sancta Maria, through which the Word took flesh. Her submission to the Divine Will - her fiat - stands as an eternal exemplar of feminine virtue and grace.

The mothers of the Old Testament, as explicated by Augustine, fortell the coming of Mary. Their faith, their struggles, and the divine intervention in their lives all point to the penultimate intervention - the Incarnation. In these women, we observe the nascent rays of the coming Dawn, they are lauded as the foremothers of the Messiah (Connolly, 2002).

Yet, Augustine's reflections convey not merely the roles of prominent biblical women, but also a deeper theological implication. In his treatise, women come to represent the

Church itself, the Bride of Christ. This nuptial imagery elucidates the reciprocal relationship between Christ the Redeemer and humanity, for it is through the Church that Christ's graces are disseminated unto the faithful.

Moreover, women in the Augustinian paradigm not only receive grace, but also are active participants in its propagation. Within the familial and societal structures of Augustine's era, women largely bore the duty of religious nurture, hence shaping early Christian formation. Augustine acknowledges this influential role, underscoring the indispensable part they play in fostering the faith of future generations.

Further, Augustine discerns in the felicitous lives of holy women—those like Monica, his own mother—a vivid allegory for the spiritual life of the believer. Monica's unceasing prayers for Augustine's conversion effloresced to fruition, emblematic of the Church's intercessory role on behalf of her children (Manz, 2004).

The penitential aspect of women's role as seen in Augustine's writings is subtler yet profound. Contrition and repentance, exemplified through the Magdalene's tears at Christ's feet, signal the turning of hearts—the metanoia—required for reconciliation with God. Their compunction is not seen as a fruit of weakness, but rather as a wellspring of authentic spiritual renewal.

In light of these contemplations, Augustine heralded women not merely as the bearers of the Original Sin but also as the instrumental bearers of redemption. The line of Eve, through the cooperative act of bearing life despite the pains of childbirth, entails an active participation in the unraveling of salvation history. Each mother, each woman, by Augustine's account, thus mirrors the hope of Eve's promised seed.

Therefore, Augustine's theological tapestry regarding women in salvation history is intricate and rich. He celebrates their integral role in the unfolding drama of redemption while recognizing the profound spiritual maternity that they exercise over the sons and daughters of the Church.

In fine, the esteemed theologian did not mince words when he avowed the necessity of studying the Old Testament figures to fully grasp the New Testament truth. Verily, the robust narrative of women in the Holy Writ serves as a testament to their indispensable role in God's salvific plan—a theme perpetuated in Augustine's devout reflections on the subject.

Nonetheless, all this pondering should never lead the faithful astray from recognizing that the ultimate salvation comes not through human merit but through divine grace alone—a grace in which women, according to Augustine, have played and continue to play a pivotal role.

Exploring the Shadows: The Dual Nature of Penance

In this exploration of penance, we delve into the juxtaposition of human frailty and divine absolution, an interplay that Augustine so intricately parsed in his theological inquiries. Penance presents itself not solely as an act of contrition but as a gateway to spiritual renaissance, where the soul, encumbered by its trespasses, finds closeness with God in the very recognition and confession of its falls. This duality of penance—as both a submission to the shadow of sin and an affirmation of the light of forgiveness—is mirrored in the beautifully paradoxical nature of Christian life, where through the embrace of one's weakness, one may be found strong in the mercy of the Father (2 Corinthians 12:10). In the sanctity of penance, the believer encounters a merciful God, whose readiness to forgive mirrors the very essence of divine Love—a central theme to Augustine's scholarship, as he journeyed through the mysteries of grace, propounded not only in scriptural exegesis but in the lived experience of the early Church (Anderson, 2002). Thus, as we venture deeper into the shadows cast by our own iniquities, may we be ever mindful of the unquenchable light that penance ushers into our hearts, a light that reveals itself all the more brightly as we acknowledge the darkness from whence it springs.

The Darkness of Sin and the Light of Forgiveness Continuing from the exploration of shadows inherent in penance, the heart now turns to a contemplation most profound: the weighty blackness of sin contrasted starkly by the refulgent illumination of divine forgiveness. This seemingly dichotomous relationship provides the scaffold for the christian soul's journey from despair to redemption, a path well trodden by saints prior, yet ever new for each penitent.

In the darkness of sin, the soul finds itself shackled, much like the prisoners in the allegory of the cave discerned by the ancients; chained, facing shadows and believing them to be the entirety of existence. Sin clouds the mind's eye, preventing it from gazing upon the Light of Truth. It's a malady that infests the heart, a corruption that severs the sinner from the lifegiving radiance of the Almighty. The wound it inflicts is deep, yea, it permeates the very fabric of being, for sin is nought but a turning away from the eternal Good, a willful descent into the abyss (Shannon, 2017).

Yet, though sin's bleak night seems impenetrable, it is pierced by the luminescent dawn of forgiveness. Forgiveness, a gracious agent of the Most High, is more than an act; 'tis a divine bestowal that renews and restores. The faith articulates this beautifully through the sacrament of penance, wherein the penitent, humbled and contrite, confesses his trespasses and receives absolution through the ministry of the Church, that blessed Bride of Christ (Rosenfield, 1963).

This concept has been mirrored in the parable of the Prodigal Son—wherein the merciful father receives his wayward child with open arms; a poignant exemplification of divine mercy's swiftness to forgive the repentant. Like the father in the parable, God's forgiveness is boundless, ready to reconcile the sinner who returns from distant lands of sin and spiritual destitution.

It is significant to delve into the nature of forgiveness. Forgiveness, in its purest form, is not mere forgetfulness nor is it a simple pardon. In essence, it is a re-creation, an act that reestablishes the ruptured relationship between Creator and creature. It's akin to the breaking of dawn, which does not just dispel darkness but initiates a new day; thus, forgiveness brings forth a new creation, a soul reborn (Norris, 2003).

To receive forgiveness is to be bathed in light unblemished. In this brilliant aura, the soul is called to reflect upon its transgressions and emerge metamorphosed, transfigured by grace. This divine light does not serve to condemn but to invite the soul to a higher calling, a restoration to its pristine state before its fall into sin's shadow.

However, the journey from the dungeons of sin into the liberating light of forgiveness is fraught with travail. As the creature confronts its darkness, a profound sorrow takes hold— this sorrow, though bitter, proves salvific, for 'tis the gateway to true repentance. Properly understood, this dolor is not just a lamentation over sin, but a sorrow for having offended the highest good, by preferring lesser goods (Manz, 2004).

In pursuit of absolution, the soul must exhibit authentic contrition which is no mere remorse of fear, but a sorrow borne of love. And with an act of the will, it turns from the beguiling lures of sin to embrace the austere yet beautiful path of virtue, resolving to avoid the near occasions of sin henceforth.

Penance plays a vital role in this transformation. As the creature reflects upon its failings, penance acts as a curative discipline. Through self-denial and acts of charity, the person cooperates with grace to repair the damage caused by their offenses—a restitution not only to God but to the natural order which sin has marred.

The Sacrament of Penance thus stands as an ineffable gift, a sacrament where heaven meets earth in a delicate dance of justice and mercy. The penitent, through the absolution imparted by the priest, is submerged in the font of forgiveness. The priest acts in persona Christi, a conduit for the mercy of the Redeemer, the one who took upon Himself the weight of human iniquity (Thompson, 1948).

Forgiveness is a phenomenon that may yet baffle the intellect, for its generosity defies the economy of human justice. It does not oblige the penitent to recompense equal to the offense, but rather infuses the soul with grace sufficient to overcome the vestiges of sin. In this divine gesture, the sinner experiences the liberating truth that in God's kingdom, love triumphs over law, and mercy rejoices against judgment.

Thus reconciled, the penitent re-enters the fellowship of the faithful, the body of Christ, where the light of forgiveness perpetually shines. The communal aspect of forgiveness is pivotal, for sin does not merely isolate the individual from God but from the congregation of believers. The absolved are henceforth called to be lanterns unto others, bearing witness to the grace that transformed them, dispelling the darkness in the world around (Pratt,
1903).

Through the grace-filled process of repentance and forgiveness, individuals are not only restored but are also sanctified. They are refined like silver, emerging from the refiner's fire with a lustrous sheen, ready to engage more fully in the divine life. In this sanctification,
God brings good out of evil, demonstrating His power to write straight with crooked lines.

In the perpetual tension between the darkness of sin and the light of forgiveness, there lies a profound narrative of human frailty and divine sovereignty. The transparent truth reveals itself that no depth of sin can ever exceed the magnitude of God's forgiveness. For every soul encased in shadow, forgiveness stands ready to cast forth a resplendent light that heralds a new beginning.

Augustine's Insights on Divine Mercy

As the discourse on penitence deepens, let us turn with intent to the discernments of Augustine, for in his erudition, we find the plenteous springs of Divine Mercy. His musings are as rays of light that pierce through the dark shroud of sin, revealing the resplendent visage of a forgiving God. Augustine, with a past marred by transgressions of his own, became a vessel of profound understanding regarding the vastness of God's merciful embrace.

Beneath the weighty cloak of original sin, Augustine discerned the redemptive power bestowed by the Almighty. In the dolorous throes of his confessions, there unearths the tender-hearted whisper of God's compassion (Augustine, 398). He perceived that the great provider of mercy is none other than the Creator Himself, showering His creatures with unmeasured scions of grace. Wistfully he ponders, in his written tomes, the manner in which divine mercy touches the penitent soul and transforms it from the chaff of sin into golden shoots of virtue.

Augustine's theological insights illuminate the essence of God's merciful actions; they are not solely a response to sin, but are an ever-present offering—constantly flowing forth. As the brook nourishes the valley, so does mercy invigorate the soul parched by iniquity (Augustine et al., 1955). He articulates that divine mercy extends beyond the bounds of temporality, enveloping the sinner before the act of contrition is even uttered, preparing the ground for repentance's seed.

Moreover, Augustine extolled the magnanimity of God's mercy in the economy of salvation. Every page of salvation history is saturated in the ink of God's clemency. What greater testament to this than the incarnation of Christ, Whom Augustine venerates as the embodiment of this divine attribute? Christ, the intercessor, stands as a testament to the extent of mercy's reach — bridging the expanse between the divine and fallen humanity.

In the writings of Augustine, one descries the notion that mercy is not simply an act of God but rather an extension of His very being. It is in the character of the Almighty to be merciful, as it is the sun's character to emanate warmth and light. God's mercy, hence, cannot be exhausted, for it is as infinite as His nature; as we are made in His image, we are called to mirror this mercy in our own feeble way.

Upon this pilgrimage through sin and forgiveness, Augustine heralds the transformative power of Divine Mercy. It is this divine benevolence that catalyzes the metamorphosis of the sinner's heart. Even the most hardened of hearts, when softened by the gentle touch of mercy, can become as the fertile loam, ripe for sowing seeds of righteousness (Augustine, 426).

Critical in Augustine's musings is the idea that mercy avails itself
most abundantly to the humble. The Almighty's mercy cascades
like a mighty deluge upon those who recognize their lowliness
and bereavement without His grace (Augustine, 413). Thus,
humility is exalted as a virtue prerequisite to the reception of
this most holy benevolence.

It cannot be overlooked that Augustine positions the Church as
the indispensable channel of such divine mercy. The sacraments,
particularly that of Reconciliation, are enriched by God's
forgiveness, which is dispensed through the hands of His
ministers. Augustine solemnly teaches that it is within this
sacred ambit that the divine dispensation of mercy is made most
manifest to the fallen (Augustine et al., 1955).

Let us recall that, for Augustine, mercy's wellspring is Love. Ever
does he delineate the two as intertwined; mercy is the
handmaiden of charity, its flow stemming from the heart replete
with divine love. For in mercy, there is a recognition of the
other's dignity, and in love, a yearning to elevate them
(Augustine, 401).

Even in the murk of temptation, Augustine finds a reflection of
Divine Mercy at work. He holds that in permitting temptation,
God crafts an opportunity for souls to cleave more firmly to Him,
thus drawing from the wells of mercy more deeply than ever

before. Temptation becomes not a fall into the abyss, but a leap into the arms of an ever-ready Savior (Augustine, 426).

In this same vein, Augustine sees in suffering a divine tool—conducive to an awareness of our need for God's merciful aid. Afflictions are thereby transmuted into occasions for mercy, birthing in the believer a beautiful depravity—a poverty of spirit that makes room for the expanse of divine generosity (Augustine, 395).

Divine Mercy, as conveyed by Augustine, is not to be hoarded but shared. He calls the faithful to act as conduits of this mercy, to forgive as they are forgiven, reflecting the boundless capacity for pardon inherent in the divine (Augustine, 408). This practice of interspersed mercy knits a tapestry of forgiveness upon which the community of believers may tread tenderly.

Thus, Augustine portrays the ultimate destiny of the soul as one intertwined with Divine Mercy. He illumines that in the cosmic dance of creation, redemption, and final glorification, mercy plays the pivotal role that enables souls to participate fully in the divine life. It is the golden strand that ties the finite to the Infinite (Augustine, 413).

In his contemplations, Augustine has unfurled a panorama of Divine Mercy that stretches from the furthest reaches of eternity to the most intimate whispers of the heart. His insights remain a beacon for all who navigate the tumultuous seas of sin and seek the harbor of God's merciful grace.

Chapter 7: The Gift of Ashes: Embracing our Mortality

In our preceding discourse, we didst wander through the dimly lit corridors of penance, whereat the soul, led by God's meritorious grace, embraceth the darkness of sin only to emerge into the resplendent light of forgiveness. Turning the page, let us now ponder the incontrovertible foundation upon which this transformative sojourn doth rest; our own mortality. The essence and import of ashes, as Augustine hath so aptly preached, remain a somber yet potent reminder of our ephemeral nature, and within this realization lieth our ultimate liberation. For as the dust returneth to the earth as it was, so the spirit returneth unto the God who gave it – a truth that both humbles and exalts the human condition (Ecclesiastes 12:7). Through the penitential lens bestowed by the age-old practice of adorning oneself with ashes, we are invited to delve into the profound recognition that from the very ashes of our temporal form, a gateway to eternity standeth ever ajar.

The Symbolism of Ashes in Augustine's Thought In the profound contemplations of Augustine, ashes arise not only as mere detritus of the physical realm but as emblematic of a profound spiritual truth. This truth, woven intricately through the fabric of divine revelation, beckons the soul to a recognition of its temporal state and its potential for renewal in the hands of the Creator. Within these ashes, there lies a duality — a reminder of the humility bestowed upon humanity and a symbol of penitential sorrow that precedes the joy of absolution.

Augustine, in his voluminous discourses, marks the ashes as the dust from whence humanity was sculpted, serving as an ever-present memento of the origin and end of mortal life. "Remember that thou art dust, and to dust thou shalt return" — this solemn admonition echoes throughout the narrative of repentance (Genesis 3:19). As the worshippers don the ashen cross upon their brows, they embody Augustine's pervasive theme: a return to the humus, the earth, in acknowledgment of their earthly nature.

To delve into the ashes is to delve into a narrative of fall and redemption. Augustine elucidates the ashes as testimony to the fall of Adam, wherein humanity's antique glory was reduced to mere ash. Yet, it's in this reduction that a pathway to redemption is manifest. The ashes, then, are not merely the end, but the very medium through which reconciliation with the Divine may commence.

Moreover, Augustine perceives in the sacramental use of ashes a call to penance. In the deliberate act of smearing ashes on oneself, one embraces a penitential posture, akin to the ancient Israelites donning sackcloth and sitting amidst ashes in times of mourning and repentance (Jonah 3:6). Thus, the ashes emerge as a sacramental sign, an outward token of an inward contrition and the transformative work of God's grace.

In the solemn rite of Ash Wednesday, the ashes stirred upon the crown of the faithful serve as a mark of mortality. This tradition is deeply rooted in a sentiment that Augustine reverently addresses — the brevity of life and the fleeting nature of worldly pursuits. As the ash is to the fire that has consumed, so is the life of mortals to the eternality of God.

This symbolism extends beyond personal penitence, reaching into the communal aspects of the Church. Augustine's thought posits that just as the ashes are gathered collectively from the remnants of the Palm Sunday celebration, so are the faithful called to unite in their acknowledgement of sinfulness and need for grace. The community, thus united, finds strength in shared humility and collective supplication.

The ashen cross imprinted upon the brow also stands as a silent testament to the hope that lies beyond penance. For Augustine, the very shape of the cross imbues the ashes with a redemptive quality, a foreshadowing of the Paschal mystery. It signifies that out of penitential ashes can rise the glory of resurrection — from repentance to salvation.

Augustine's reflections resonate with the belief that through the ashes, the Divine Potter reshapes the marred vessel of humanity. The ashes are a starting point, a canvas upon which the narrative of grace is to be painted. They signal not an end, but a beginning — a summons to spiritual rebirth and restoration.

The application of ashes likewise confronts the temptation of vanity. As Augustine frequently expounds, the human heart is prone to the seduction of earthly fame and beauty.

The imposition of the ashen cross speaks against this, inviting the soul to seek beauty not in the flesh, which fades, but in the spirit, which endures.

Weighty yet hopeful is the message carried by the ashes in Augustine's doctrine. They are a token of God's justice, a reminder of the righteous judgement that all must face. But intertwined with this solemnity is the golden thread of divine mercy. Augustine experiences in the ashes a paternal chastisement that begets healing, a sorrow that yields to joy.

Within the Lenten observance, the ashes serve as the threshold to a journey. Augustine's commentary on this transformative pilgrimage from the ashes of Ash Wednesday to the dawn of

Easter Sunday teems with a recognition of the cyclical nature of Christian life — from death comes life, from despair rises hope.

Herein, Augustine sees an eschatological dimension to the symbolism of the ashes. They are not merely about remembering one's earthly mortality but also about anticipating the eternal life that Christ promises. The ashes ennoble the faithful with a vision of their heavenly destiny, thereby infusing their temporal lives with meaningful purpose.

Yet, amidst these meditations, one must not overlook the personal dimension compelling the heart towards sanctity. For Augustine, the ashes are an intimate call to each believer, a summons to forsake sin and embrace a sanctified existence through ceaseless conversion, prayer, and acts of charity.

Thus, the profound symbolism of ashes within Augustine's thought encapsulates a complex interplay of humility, penance, mortality, communal identity, and eschatological hope. It weaves an intricate theology of human frailty confronted with divine mercy — a theology etched upon the very foreheads of the faithful as they embark upon the Lenten voyage.

The Transformative Journey from Ashes to Easter's Dawn

The solemn observance of Ash Wednesday ushers in the Lenten season, a period that serves both as a testament to mortality and a preparatory passage toward the
Resurrection's light. Ashes, symbolic of penance and contrition, lay upon the brows of the devout, conversely heralding both an end and an earnest beginning.

In this sacred interval, the heart, akin to fallow ground, is turned over, that it may be made ready to receive the seeds of new spiritual growth. This transformative journey, a pilgrimage of the soul, beckons the faithful to traverse from the shadowed valley of sin to the dawn of Easter's jubilation. The path is one of solemn reflection, voluntary mortification, and quiet anticipation.

Hath it not been said within the annals of sacred doctrine that from dust man was formed, and to dust shall he return? The remembrance of this foundational truth is stark upon Ash Wednesday, stark upon the visage of each Christian soul (Genesis 3:19). Recall, for it is written in holy writ, each man must ponder his own transitory nature and thus, apprehend the seeming frailty of his mortal coil.

Yet, within this visceral acknowledgment of our earthly demise, therein burgeons a resplendent hope. For through the descent into dust, humanity may verily ascend in the spirit, reborn through penitential sacrifice and divine grace. The binding twine of human sin falls away as the soul, chastened by ash, emerges anew.

The penitential journey is bespeckled with many a trial and tear, much as our Blessed

Mother Mary experienced a sorrow that pierced her heart like a sword (Luke 2:35). Her sorrow, emblematic of the ashen cross, intertwines with the fabric of Lent, and in this sacred sorrowing, we find a model of purest love and unwavering faith.

As wayfarers of the spirit, we embrace the rigors of Lent not as a singular practice of forsaking earthly pleasures but rather as a profound engagement with the divine reality. It is through this forsaking, this glorious surrender, that souls are enkindled with a flame that not even the dark of death can extinguish.

Await with bated breath the wondrous dawn of Easter, wherein the love most high triumphs over the tomb's desolation. This holy culmination affords to the wearied pilgrim a spectacle of life's indomitable persistence, life that bursts forth from the tomb as brilliantly as the morning star dispels night's velvet cloak.

The sacrament of reconciliation stands as a beacon during these forty days. As the confessional becomes the sacred forge where the soul, alloyed with divine mercy, is reshaped. In the act of confessing, the penitent enacts a spiritual resurrection, emerging absolved, like Christ who rose victorious, shattering the chains of Hades (Lowenstein, 2002).

Embrace the disciplines of fasting, prayer, and almsgiving, instructed as necessary to the Christian experience by the Savior Himself (Matthew 6:1-18). These pious exercises, imbued with a spirit of genuine conversion, lend a rhythm to the Lenten journey, a rhythm that throbs with the heartbeat of the Church itself.

Verily, the fire of this pilgrimage is not merely one that consumes but one that illumines and warms, guiding the penitent through the night's darkness. Through the gauntlet of temptation and soul-searching, the radiant morning of the Resurrection beckons. Lo, the paschal candle flickers as the herald of this celestial morning, the light of Christ piercing through the shroud of the penitential season.

Consider the theological efficacy of Lent's conclusion. The passion, death, and the Resurrection of Christ are relived and celebrated in every facet of the Triduum. From the solemnity of Maundy Thursday to the mournful silence of Good Friday, culminating in the hallowed Vigil of Easter, the believer embarks on a liturgical sojourn that mirrors the salvific trajectory of humankind.

Through the juxtaposition of ash and the Easter morn, the Church demonstrates a masterful understanding of the human condition—the perpetual oscillation between sin and redemption, death and life. It is this mystery that is presented to the believer, a profound truth upon which to meditate and draw wisdom (Jay, 1998).

Thus, the transformation from Ash Wednesday to Easter Sunday captures the very quintessence of Lent, a season impersonating life's grand masquerade, at once filled with both the bitter and the sublime. The transience of ashes gives way to the imperishable joy of Easter; from penitential sorrow springs eternal bliss.

In reflection of this Lenten tapestry, one perceives an elegant symmetry, a delicate balance between the temporality of the flesh and the immortality of the soul. Within the context of the sacred tradition, this excursus upon Lent offers a lens through which the divine economy of salvation is perceived, contemplated, and ultimately, profoundly revered.

Let then this holy Lenten season be a testament to the resiliency of faith, to the transformation that beckons each soul from the ashes of human frailty to the dawn of a renewed existence. Thus do we encompass the full arc of penance to jubilation, with each step upon this path drawing us nearer to the ineffable light of the Risen One.

Augustine's Legacy for Today's Faithful

As the final leaves of this book's chapters turn, it can't be overstated how the shadow of Augustine, that prodigious doctor of the Church, still stretches across the centuries to touch the hearts of today's faithful. His deep contemplation and profound insights continue to act as a beacon of understanding, rekindling the embers of faith in the elegiac blend of darkness and light, sin and salvation which characterizes the human condition.

In an era fraught with confusion and myriad quests for meaning, Augustine remains relevant, resonating with those yearning for truth and authenticity in their spiritual journey. The weight of his scholarship and the extent of his influence are as a great tome upon the lectern of history, the pages of which endless seekers may turn for guidance.

We may reflect upon how his interpretations of penitence offer a salutary path through the tribulations of contemporary life. His thoughts on Ash Wednesday, underscored by the symbolic imposition of ashes, seem to whisper to us of the humility and remembrance that today's world sorely needs. Augustine's vision compels us to confront our own transience and encourages the embracing of our shared mortality.

Moreover, Augustine's assimilation of Jewish wisdom, as presented in the tapestry of our faith's rich history, campaigns for an inclusive understanding, prompting us to look back as we move forward. His recognition of the archetypes of penance serves to illuminate layers of meaning that continue to unfold within scripture's living words for the adherent earnest in contemplation.

The patriarch Abraham's sojourn, which Augustine so eloquently exegetes, guides us in our struggle to harmonize the divine will with our own frail ambitions. That struggle, mirrored in the dilemma of today's believers, walks hand-in-hand with the desire to cultivate a humility akin to that of the father of many nations.

And how shall we speak of Mary, the indelible icon of sorrow and strength? Augustine's reflections upon her lament bind her irrevocably to our Lenten experience. The seven dolors, entwined with the abiding symbol of the ashen cross, lay bare the path from personal grief to redemptive grace.

The history of sin and salvation, so artfully delineated by Augustine, from the tears shed by Eve to those at the foot of the Cross, weaves a narrative that speaks just as poignantly to modern souls as it did to early Christians. The role of women, central to this narrative, is one which Augustine contemplates with profound reverence and theological acumen, rendering unto Mary and Eve their due in salvation's grand design.

Within the paradoxical nature of penance, Augustine roots a duality that aptly encapsulates the Christian experience: to live ever in the world, yet not of it. His meditations on sin, a darkness so pervasive, are lit by the relentless flame of divine mercy. It's a lesson that teaches us to seek forgiveness with the same vigor we must apply in our efforts to offer it.

The symbolism of ashes holds a transformative power in Augustine's thought. Such a symbol, denoting both end and beginning, death and renewal, reflects the inexorable cycle from Ash Wednesday to the dawn of Easter. It's a journey of renewal that the faithful of today are called to traverse with intention and hope.

In closing, Augustine's legacy endures as a testament to the unbroken dialogue between humanity and the divine. It's a legacy that resonates with the lived experience of each believer, speaking to the core of what it means to navigate existence with faith as one's compass. Such wisdom, such guidance, is a treasure beyond reckoning, a lamp for the feet of those traveling the oft-veiled paths of our world.

Let us then hold fast to the lessons imparted by this venerable saint, using them to cultivate a faith that is living and active, characterized not merely by an assiduous nod to tradition but invigorated by the sincere striving after holiness and wisdom. Augustine's legacy instructs us to approach the divine mysteries with a blend of intellectua

Appendix A: Selected Prayers and

Sermons for Ash Wednesday

In the observance of Ash Wednesday, the faithful are beckoned to the solemnity of the Lenten season, a time for introspection and penance. This appendix gathers devotions and discourses that invite contemplation on the mortal state of man, the depth of God's boundless mercy, and the path to spiritual renewal.

1. Prayer for Penitence and Renewal

O most gracious and merciful Lord, Thou who art cloaked in mystery, yet present in the sojourn of our earthly pilgrimage, look upon Thy servants gathered in humble acknowledgment of our frailty. As we are marked with ashes, a symbol of our creation and our fall, kindle within us a flame of repentance. Render our hearts contrite that we might be made anew in thine image and likeness. We seek refuge in Thy boundless compassion, trusting in the salvation wrought by Thy holy sacrifice. Amen.

2. Sermon Excerpt: "The Dust from which We Came"

In the penitential season dost we ponder the truth that from
dust we were made, and to dust we shall return. This terrestrial
form is but transient, and all earthly vanities crumble as does
the ash. Yet, it is in this humility we recall our everlasting spirit,
molded by divine breath, yearning to return to its Creator. Our
dispositions, thus sullied by the blemishes of sin, seek to be
cleansed through His benevolence that the ash of our iniquity
may give rise to the lustrous diamond of grace.

3. Litany for Ash Wednesday

Ashes to ashes, dust to dust; Lord, in Thy mercy, hear our
prayer. Grant us wisdom to discern truth, courage to confess our
trespasses, strength to forsake our wayward courses, and
humility to wear the ash as a crown of penitence. May we
witness to the hope that lies within, assured by the Blessed
Mother's intercession, as we embark on this trek to
resurrection. Through the travail of these forty days, prepare us
to greet with joy the Paschal mystery. Amen.

In crafting these reverent articulations of faith, may they serve
to focus the mind and uplift the spirit, drawing the faithful into a

deeper communion with the divine throughout this solemn season and beyond.

References

1.   Pratt, J. B. (1903). The Ethics of St. Augustine. *The International Journal of Ethics*, *13*(2), 222-235.

2.   Kaufman, P. I. (1982). *Augustinian Piety and Catholic Reform: Augustine, Colet, and Erasmus*. Mercer University Press.

3.   Augustine et al. (1955). "Augustine: Earlier Writings." The Library of Christian Classics: Ichthus Edition.

4.   Augustine. (1961). Confessions. R. S. Pine-Coffin (Trans.). Penguin Books.

5.   Augustine. (395). "The Confessions of Saint Augustine."

6.   Augustine. (397). Confessions.

7.   Augustine. (398). "On Christian Doctrine."

8.   Augustine. (400). Letters.

9.   Augustine. (401). "Letters of St. Augustine."

10. Augustine. (408). "The City of God."

11. Augustine. (413). "Enchiridion on Faith, Hope, and Love."

12. Augustine. (426). "Retractions."

13. Augustine. (426). City of God.

14.   Connell, M. (1998, September). Ash Wednesday: meaning and history. In *Journal of the Liturgical Conference* (Vol. 15, No. 1, pp. 7-14). Taylor & Francis Group.

15.   Ferguson, J. (1979). Ash Wednesday. *English Studies in Africa*, *22*(2), 99-110.

16.   Screech, M. A. (1990). Echoes of Saint Augustine in Rabelais. In *Augustine, the Harvest, and Theology (1300-1650)* (pp. 286-299). Brill.

17.   Thompson, A. H. (1948). Classical echoes in Medieval authors. *History*, *33*(117/118), 29-48.

18.   Lowenstein, S. M. (2002). *The Jewish cultural tapestry: International Jewish folk traditions.* Oxford University Press.

19.   Cardin, N. B. (2000). *The Tapestry of Jewish Time: A Spiritual Guide to Holidays and Life-Cycle Events*. Behrman House, Inc.

20.   Neusner, J. (2004). *The Talmud: A close encounter*. Wipf and Stock Publishers.

21.   Matthews, G. B. (2020). Augustine. In *Encyclopedia of Medieval Philosophy: Philosophy between 500 and 1500* (pp. 225-232). Dordrecht: Springer Netherlands.

22.   Norris Jr, R. A. (2003). Augustine and the Close of the Ancient Period of Interpretation. *A history of biblical interpretation*, *1*, 380-408.

23. Genesis. (n.d.). In The Holy Bible, King James Version.

24. Genesis. (n.d.). The Holy Bible, King James Version. Retrieved March 10, 2023, from https://www.biblegateway.com/passage/?search=Genesis+3%3A19

25. Holy Bible, King James Version. (2017). Zondervan.

26.   Bucur, B. G. (2008). AUGUSTINE'S DE TRINITATE. *St Vladimirs Theological Quarterly*, *521*, 67-93.

27.   Kim, W. J. (1991). *Reconciliation as a psychological and theological reality: a comparison between Carl G. Jung and Paul J. Tillich*. University of Ottawa (Canada).

28.   Almén, B. (2003). Narrative archetypes: A critique, theory, and method of narrative analysis. *Journal of Music Theory*, *47*(1), 1-39.

29.   Bancroft, G. (1866). *Memorial Address on the Life and Character of Abraham Lincoln: Delivered, at the Request of Both Houses of the Congress of America, Before Them, in the House of Representatives at Washington, on the 12th of February, 1866.* US Government Printing Office.

30.   Cowley, A. (1881). *The complete works in verse and prose of Abraham Cowley: now for the first time collected and edited: with memorial introduction and notes and illustrations, portraits, etc* (Vol. 2). T. and A. Constable] Printed for private circulation.

31.   Norten, M. (2024). *Our Redemptive Journey: Pictured in the Lives of the Patriarchs*. Christian Faith Publishing, Inc..

32.   Jay, N. (1988). Sacrifice, descent and the patriarchs. *Vetus Testamentum*, *38*(Fasc. 1), 52-70.

33.   Cameron, M. (2012). *Christ meets me everywhere: Augustine's early figurative exegesis.* Oxford University Press.

34.   Levering, M. (2013). *The theology of Augustine: An introductory guide to his most important works.* Baker Books.

35.   Ewing, J. (2016). *From Grief to Grace: The Journey from Tragedy to Triumph.* Sophia Institute Press.

36.   Finley, K. (2004). *The Liturgy of Motherhood: Moments of Grace.* Sheed & Ward.

37.   Jones, N. A. (1997). By Woman's Tears Redeemed: Female Lament in St. Augustine's Confessions and the Correspondence of Abelard and Heloise. *Sex and Gender in Medieval and Renaissance Texts: The Latin Tradition*, 15-39.

38.   Gertsman, E. (Ed.). (2012). *Crying in the Middle Ages: Tears of history.* Routledge.

39.   Onongha, K. (2013). Suffering, Salvation, and the Sovereignty of God: Towards a Theology of Suffering. *Journal of Adventist Mission Studies*, *9*(2), 126-136.

40.   Satterfield, B. (2001). Gethsemane and Golgotha: Why and What the Savior Suffered. *The Book of Mormon and the message of the Four Gospels*, 173-200.

41.   van Bavel, T. J. (1997). Maternal aspects in salvation history according to Augustine. *Augustiniana*, *47*(3/4), 251-290.

42.   Connolly, W. E. (2002). *The Augustinian imperative: A reflection on the politics of morality*. Rowman & Littlefield Publishers.

43.   Rosenfield, C. (1963). The shadow within: The conscious and unconscious use of the double. *Daedalus*, 326-344.

44.   Van der Merwe, D. G. (2014). Early Christian spiritualities of sin and forgiveness according to 1 John. *HTS: Theological Studies*, *70*(1), 1-11.

45.   McInerney, J. J. (2017). The greatness of humility: St Augustine on moral excellence.

46.   Schneiderman, L. (2008). *Embracing our mortality: Hard choices in an age of medical miracles*. Oxford University Press.

47.   O'Connell, R. J. (1996). *Images of conversion in St. Augustine's Confessions*. Fordham Univ Press.

48.	Manz, B. (2004). *Paradise in ashes: A Guatemalan journey of courage, terror, and hope* (Vol. 8). Univ of California Press.

49.	Anderson, D. R. (2002). The Soteriological Impact of Augustine's Change from Premillennialism to Amillennialism: Part One.". *Journal of the Grace Evangelical Society*, *15*(28), 25-36.

50.	Shannon, M. (2017). *According to Your Mercy: Praying with the Psalms from Ash Wednesday to Easter.* Paraclete Press.

THE 15 PRAYERS OF ST. BRIDGET

These Prayers and these Promises have been copied from a book printed in Toulouse in 1740 and published by the P. Adrien Parvilliers of the Company of Jesus, Apostolic Missionary of the Holy Land, with approbation, permission and recommendation to distribute them.
Pope Pius IX took cognisance of these Prayers with the prologue; he approved them May 31, 1862, recognising them as true and for the good of souls.

As St. Bridget for a long time wanted to know the number of blows Our Lord received during His Passion, He one day appeared to her and said: "I received 5480 blows on My Body. If you wish to honour them in some way, say 15 Our Fathers and 15 Hail Marys with the following Prayers (which He taught her) for a whole year. When the year is up, you will have honoured each one of My Wounds."

He made the following promises to anyone who recited these Prayers for a whole year:

1. I will deliver 15 souls of his lineage from Purgatory.
2. 15 souls of his lineage will be confirmed and preserved in grace.
3. 15 sinners of his lineage will be converted.
4. Whoever recites these Prayers will attain the first degree of perfection.
5. 15 days before his death I will give him My Precious Body in order that he may escape eternal starvation; I will give him My Precious Blood to drink lest he thirst eternally.
6. 15 days before his death he will feel a deep contrition for all his sins and will have a perfect knowledge of them.
7. I will place before him the sign of My Victorious Cross for his help and defence against the attacks of his enemies.

8. Before his death I shall come with My Dearest
    Beloved Mother.

9. I shall graciously receive his soul, and will lead it into
    eternal joys.

10. And having led it there I shall give him a special
    draught from the fountain of My Deity, something I
    will not for those who have not recited My Prayers.

11. Let it be known that whoever may have been living
    in a state of mortal sin for 30 years, but who will
    recite devoutly, or have the intention to recite these
    Prayers, the Lord will forgive him all his sins.

12. I shall protect him from strong temptations.

13. I shall preserve and guard his 5 senses.

14. I shall preserve him from a sudden death.

15. His soul will be delivered from eternal death.

16. He will obtain all he asks for from God and the
    Blessed Virgin.

17. If he has lived all his life doing his own will and he is
    to die the next day, his life will be prolonged.

18. Every time one recites these Prayers he gains 100
    days indulgence.

19. He is assured of being joined to the supreme Choir
    of Angels.

20. Whoever teaches these Prayers to another, will have continuous joy and merit which will endure eternally.

21. There where these Prayers are being said or will be said in the future God is present with His grace.

Each prayer is preceded by one Our Father and one Hail Mary.

Our Father, who art in heaven, hallowed be thy name.
Thy kingdom come.
Thy will be done on earth as it is in heaven.
Give us this day our daily bread and forgive us our
trespasses as we forgive those who trespass against us and
lead us not into temptation but deliver us from evil. **Amen**

Hail Mary, full of grace, the Lord is with thee; blessed art
thou among women and blessed is the fruit of thy womb,
Jesus.
Holy Mary, Mother of God, pray for us sinners, now and at
the hour of our death. **Amen.**

FIRST PRAYER
Our Father - Hail Mary.
O Jesus Christ! Eternal Sweetness to those who love Thee,
joy surpassing all joy and all desire, Salvation and Hope of

all sinners, Who hast proved that Thou hast no greater
desire than to be among men, even assuming human nature
at the fullness of time for the love of men, recall all the
sufferings Thou hast endured from the instant of Thy
conception, and especially during Thy Passion, as it was
decreed and ordained from all eternity in the Divine plan.

Remember, O Lord, that during the Last Supper with Thy
disciples, having washed their feet, Thou gavest them Thy
Most Precious Body and Blood, and while at the same time
thou didst sweetly console them, Thou didst foretell them
Thy coming Passion.
Remember the sadness and bitterness which Thou didst
experience in Thy Soul as Thou Thyself bore witness saying:
"My Soul is sorrowful even unto death."

Remember all the fear, anguish and pain that Thou didst
suffer in Thy delicate Body before the torment of the
Crucifixion, when, after having prayed three times, bathed in
a sweat of blood, Thou wast betrayed by Judas, Thy disciple,
arrested by the people of a nation Thou hadst chosen and
elevated, accused by false witnesses, unjustly judged by
three judges during the flower of Thy youth and during the
solemn Paschal season.

Remember that Thou wast despoiled of Thy garments and clothed in those of derision; that Thy Face and Eyes were veiled, that Thou wast buffeted, crowned with thorns, a reed placed in Thy Hands, that Thou was crushed with blows and overwhelmed with affronts and outrages.
In memory of all these pains and sufferings which Thou didst endure before Thy Passion on the Cross, grant me before my death true contrition, a sincere and entire confession, worthy satisfaction and the remission of all my sins. **Amen.**

SECOND PRAYER
Our Father - Hail Mary.
O Jesus! True liberty of angels, Paradise of delights, remember the horror and sadness which Thou didst endure when Thy enemies, like furious lions, surrounded Thee, and by thousands of insults, spits, blows, lacerations and other unheard-of-cruelties, tormented Thee at will.

In consideration of these torments and insulting words, I beseech Thee, O my Saviour, to deliver me from all my enemies, visible and invisible, and to bring me, under Thy protection, to the perfection of eternal salvation. **Amen.**

THIRD PRAYER

Our Father - Hail Mary.

O Jesus! Creator of Heaven and earth Whom nothing can encompass or limit, Thou Who dost enfold and hold all under Thy Loving power, remember the very bitter pain.

Thou didst suffer when the Jews nailed Thy Sacred Hands and Feet to the Cross by blow after blow with big blunt nails, and not finding Thee in a pitiable enough state to satisfy their rage, they enlarged Thy Wounds, and added pain to pain, and with indescribable cruelty stretched Thy Body on the Cross, pulled Thee from all sides, thus dislocating Thy Limbs.

I beg of Thee, O Jesus, by the memory of this most Loving suffering of the Cross, to grant me the grace to fear Thee and to Love Thee. **Amen.**

FOURTH PRAYER

Our Father – Hail Mary.

O Jesus! Heavenly Physician, raised aloft on the Cross to heal our wounds with Thine, remember the bruises which Thou didst suffer and the weakness of all Thy Members which were distended to such a degree that never was there pain like unto Thine.

From the crown of Thy Head to the Soles of Thy Feet there
was not one spot on Thy Body that was not in torment, and
yet, forgetting all Thy sufferings, Thou didst not cease to
pray to Thy Heavenly Father for Thy enemies, saying:
"Father forgive them for they know not what they do."

Through this great Mercy, and in memory of this suffering,
grant that the remembrance of Thy Most Bitter Passion may
effect in us a perfect contrition and the remission of all our
sins. **Amen**.

FIFTH PRAYER
Our Father - Hail Mary.
O Jesus! Mirror of eternal splendour, remember the sadness
which Thou experienced, when contemplating in the light of
Thy Divinity the predestination of those who would be saved
by the merits of Thy Sacred Passion.

Thou didst see at the same time, the great multitude of
reprobates who would be damned for their sins, and Thou
didst complain bitterly of those hopeless lost and
unfortunate sinners.

Through this abyss of compassion and pity, and especially through the goodness which Thou displayed to the good thief when Thou saidst to him: "This day, thou shalt be with Me in Paradise." I beg of Thee, O Sweet Jesus, that at the hour of my death, Thou wilt show me mercy. **Amen**.

SIXTH PRAYER
Our Father – Hail Mary.
O Jesus! Beloved and most desirable King, remember the grief Thou didst suffer, when naked and like a common criminal.

Thou was fastened and raised on the Cross, when all Thy relatives and friends abandoned Thee, except Thy Beloved Mother, who remained close to Thee during Thy agony and whom Thou didst entrust to Thy faithful disciple when Thou saidst to Mary: "Woman, behold thy son!" and to St. John: "Son, behold thy Mother!"

I beg of Thee O my Saviour, by the sword of sorrow which pierced the soul of Thy holy Mother, to have compassion on me in all my affliction and tribulations, both corporal and spiritual, and to assist me in all my trials, and especially at the hour of my death. **Amen**.

SEVENTH PRAYER

Our Father – Hail Mary.

O Jesus! Inexhaustible Fountain of compassion, Who by a profound gesture of Love, said from the Cross: "I thirst!" suffered from the thirst for the salvation of the human race.

I beg of Thee O my Saviour, to inflame in our hearts the desire to tend toward perfection in all our acts; and to extinguish in us the concupiscence of the flesh and the ardor of worldly desires. **Amen**.

EIGHTH PRAYER

Our Father – Hail Mary.

O Jesus! Sweetness of hearts, delight of the spirit, by the bitterness of the vinegar and gall which Thou didst taste on the Cross for Love of us, grant us the grace to receive worthily.

Thy Precious Body and Blood during our life and at the hour of our death, that they may serve as a remedy and consolation for our souls. **Amen.**

NINTH PRAYER

Our Father – Hail Mary.

O Jesus! Royal virtue, joy of the mind, recall the pain Thou didst endure when, plunged in an ocean of bitterness at the approach of death, insulted, outraged by the Jews.

Thou didst cry out in a loud voice that Thou was abandoned by Thy Father, saying: "My God, My God, why hast Thou forsaken me?"

Through this anguish, I beg of Thee, O my Saviour, not to abandon me in the terrors and pains of my death. **Amen.**

TENTH PRAYER

Our Father – Hail Mary.

O Jesus! Who art the beginning and end of all things, life and virtue, remembers that for our sakes Thou was plunged in an abyss of suffering from the soles of Thy Feet to the crown of Thy Head.

In consideration of the enormity of Thy Wounds, teach me to keep, through pure love, Thy Commandments, whose way is wide and easy for those who love Thee. **Amen.**

ELEVENTH PRAYER

Our Father - Hail Mary.

O Jesus! Deep abyss of mercy, I beg of Thee, in memory of Thy Wounds which penetrated to the very marrow of Thy Bones and to the depth of Thy being, to draw me, a miserable sinner, overwhelmed by my offenses, away from sin and to hide me from Thy Face justly irritated against me, hide me in Thy wounds, until Thy anger and just indignation shall have passed away. **Amen.**

TWELFTH PRAYER

Our Father - Hail Mary.

O Jesus! Mirror of Truth, symbol of unity, bond of charity, remember the multitude of wounds with which Thou wast afflicted from head to foot, torn and reddened by the spilling of Thy adorable Blood. O great and universal pain, which Thou didst suffer in Thy virginal flesh for love of us! Sweetest Jesus! What is there that Thou couldst have done for us which Thou has not done!

May the fruit of Thy suffering be renewed in my soul by the

faithful remembrance of Thy Passion, and may Thy love
increase in my heart each day, until I see Thee in eternity:
Thou Who art the treasure of every real good and every joy,
which I beg Thee to grant me, O Sweetest Jesus, in
heaven. **Amen.**

THIRTEENTH PRAYER
Our Father - Hail Mary.
O Jesus! Strong Lion, Immortal and Invincible King,
remember the pain which Thou didst endure when all Thy
strength, both moral and physical, was entirely exhausted,
Thou didst bow Thy Head, saying: "It is consummated!"

Through this anguish and grief, I beg of Thee Lord Jesus, to
have mercy on me at the hour of my death when my mind
will be greatly troubled and my soul will be in
anguish. **Amen.**

FOURTEENTH PRAYER
Our Father - Hail Mary.
O Jesus! Only Son of the Father, Splendour and Figure of His
Substance, remember the simple and humble
recommendation.

Thou didst make of Thy Soul to Thy Eternal Father, saying:
"Father, into Thy Hands I commend My Spirit!" And with Thy
Body all torn, and Thy Heart Broken, and the bowels of
Thy Mercy open to redeem us, Thou didst Expire.

By this Precious Death, I beg of Thee O King of Saints,
comfort me and help me to resist the devil, the flesh and the
world, so that being dead to the world I may live for Thee
alone.

I beg of Thee at the hour of my death to receive me, a
pilgrim and an exile returning to Thee. **Amen.**

FIFTEENTH PRAYER
Our Father - Hail Mary.
O Jesus! True and fruitful Vine! Remember the abundant
outpouring of Blood which Thou didst so generously shed
from Thy Sacred Body as juice from grapes in a wine press.

From Thy Side, pierced with a lance by a soldier, blood and
water issued forth until there was not left in Thy Body a
single drop, and finally, like a bundle of myrrh lifted to the
top of the Cross Thy delicate Flesh was destroyed, the very

Substance of Thy Body withered, and the Marrow of Thy Bones dried up.

Through this bitter Passion and through the outpouring of Thy Precious Blood, I beg of Thee, O Sweet Jesus, to receive my soul when I am in my death agony. **Amen.**

CONCLUSION

O Sweet Jesus! Pierce my heart so that my tears of penitence and love will be my bread day and night; may I be converted entirely to Thee, may my heart be Thy perpetual habitation, may my conversation be pleasing to Thee, and may the end of my life be so praiseworthy that I may merit Heaven and there with Thy saints, praise Thee forever. **Amen.**

www.ingramcontent.com/pod-product-compliance
Lightning Source LLC
Chambersburg PA
CBHW081150130726
47996CB00009B/3065

9 798869 201935